Exeter Cathedral

A Guide for Visitors

Introduction

Welcome to Exeter Cathedral. This holy place is thought to have been a site of Christian worship since Roman times, and is still a place where prayers are said and sung every day. It is set in the midst of a lively city, not far from shops and offices, and around it everyday life goes on. But at the Cathedral the visitor comes into a different world, full of beauty and holiness.

Although there is so much to see, this is not a museum. It is a living and working place of worship and ministry, often filled with music and with many people, young and old, attending services and events.

Make your visit slowly. There are thousands of details which cannot be listed, and which you would not exhaust in a lifetime of visiting. Blue labels mark some of the main items of interest, and there are special publications on sale to help you enjoy the memorials, the rondels, and other aspects of this historic place. This guide serves to take you around the building, pausing on matters of particular interest, and to help you to go on enjoying the memory of this place even when you have left it.

We hope that whenever you recall your visit to Exeter Cathedral the memory will please you and refresh you. May God bless you.

Boy choristers singing the daily services.

The heart of the Cathedral. A priest celebrates Holy Communion in one of the chapels each day.

The ideal starting point for this book is facing the front of the Cathedral. If you decide to begin inside the Cathedral, however, turn to the section entitled *The Interior* (page 8). You may like to return to *The Cathedral in its Close* (overleaf) when you have completed your visit inside.

Numbers in the text refer to the numbers on the Cathedral plan, which can be found on the inside front cover of this guide.

The Cathedral in its Close

As you stand facing the front of the Cathedral, you will notice that it is not sited at the highest point on the hill. The huge square towers are halfway along its length, and fasten it firmly to the ground. The towers are invisible from much of the centre of the city – this is not a building that soars. The most obvious feature of the West Front is the carved stone screen, wrapped over the buttresses and pierced by the doors. The broad West Window does not tower above the screen, but spreads itself and makes the Cathedral look more squat than it is.

Long ago the Cathedral was more hemmed in than it is today. A whole row of buildings ran almost directly towards this side of the Cathedral, of which the only remnant is the trio of gabled houses behind you. The present appearance of the Cathedral Green results from a series of building removals over two hundred years. Behind the wall to the right is the Deanery, with its broad spreading roof, which was once quite invisible behind buildings now vanished. A short walk along the path beside the Deanery brings you to the ruins of the hall once used by the vicars choral – priests who used to sing the services of the Cathedral. An information board there tells you about the hall's history and what it used to look like.

More buildings stood to your left, on the north side of the Cathedral. If you visit the north tower you will see, on its side, marks left by the roof of the treasurer's house which was taken down long ago; and there were other houses beyond that, filling the corner of the Close.

There was a church on this site before the Normans built their cathedral. It stood where a cross on the grass behind you marks the site of the demolished church of St Mary Major. It was far smaller than the later Cathedral, though it was dedicated as a cathedral in the presence of Edward the Confessor in 1050, and its charter is still kept in the Cathedral's Archives. That church in turn stood where there had been an earlier Saxon monastery, where Winfrith, a local boy, came to

The Cathedral Close is often crowded with visitors enjoying this beautiful space in the middle of the city.

be educated in the seventh century. Later known as Boniface, he went as a missionary to north Germany and died for his faith. He is now one of the patron saints of Europe. All around the present West Front are the graves of the Saxons who once lived and worshipped here.

The history of the Cathedral Close goes back even further. The Saxon monastery grew up near the forum – the civic building of Roman Exeter. Burials dating from the fifth century suggest that there was Christian worship around here in the years of the Roman Empire. The memory of the Roman past was brought to life when St Mary Major church was demolished. Beneath it were the foundations for a huge military bathhouse, one of the largest in northern Europe, built in the early days of the Roman occupation of Exeter.

Nowadays, the Cathedral Green is Exeter's most beautiful space, filled on fine days by families sitting in the sun. For a thousand years, however, this cathedral close was a place of burials, and today it remains a place apart, cared for by the Cathedral. The Close was provided

(Left) Detail of carving on the West Front.

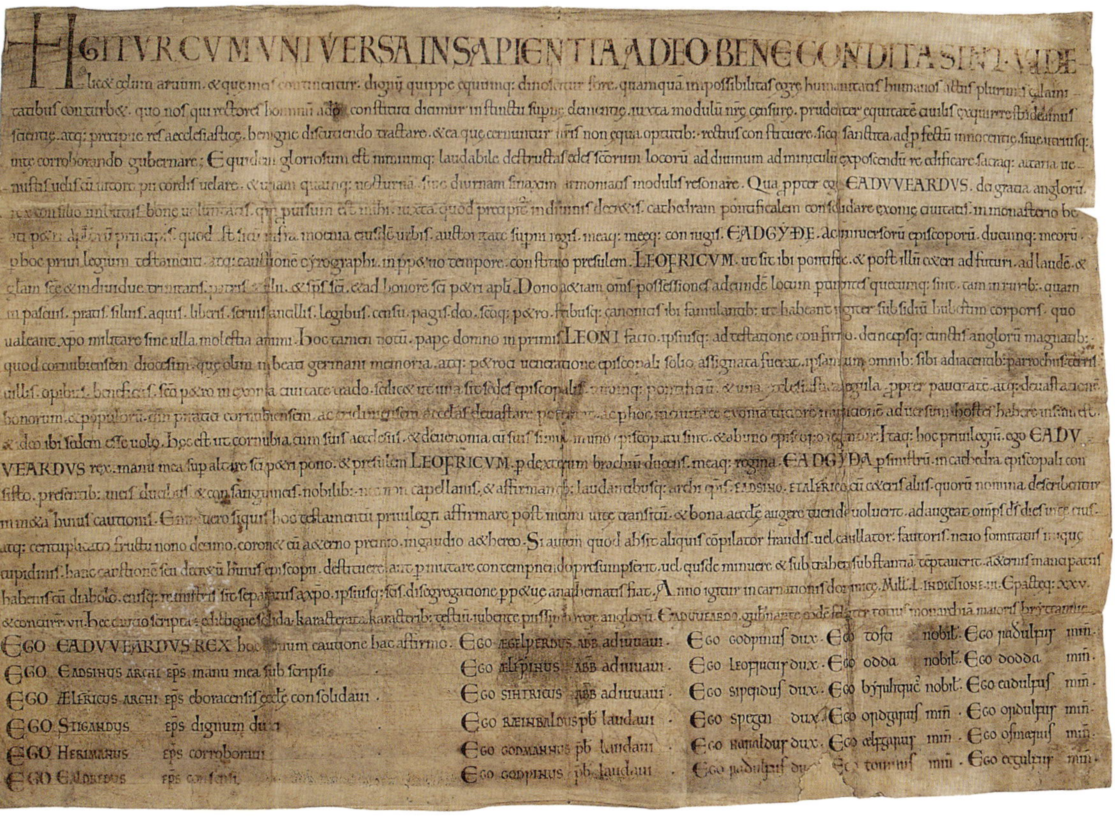

Foundation Charter of the Diocese of Exeter, 1050.

with gates in 1286 after the murder of one of the senior Cathedral clergy, Walter of Lechlade, in 1283. King Edward I visited Exeter in 1285 to settle the matter. He had the mayor and others hanged, and called the clergy to account. Today the Close continues to be the home of the Dean and three of the canons who are members of the Chapter (cathedral administrative body). Members of the Chapter come together every morning and evening to say or sing prayers, just as they have always done. The canons of Exeter were not monks. They lived in separate houses, which were grand enough to offer hospitality – and, in the case of the Deanery, worthy of royalty. The bishops of Exeter, the founders and builders of the Cathedral, left the responsibility for its daily running to the Dean and Chapter. That arrangement continues today, with the Bishop living on the opposite side of the

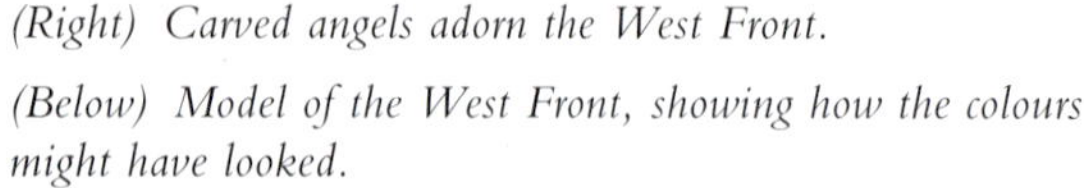

(Right) Carved angels adorn the West Front.

(Below) Model of the West Front, showing how the colours might have looked.

View of north side of the Cathedral, with St Paul's Tower on the left.

Cathedral from the canons, and coming into the Cathedral often, whether to preside formally over the diocese of Exeter from his bishop's throne, or to join in the Chapter's daily worship.

The chief entrance to the Close has always been through the Broad Gate, leading from the High Street down what are now processional steps past the County War Memorial (the work of Sir Edwin Lutyens, in 1920). This is still the route taken by distinguished visitors who come to the Cathedral, to be greeted as they enter at the Great West Door (number 1 on the plan).

The West Front of the Cathedral gives the visitor the impression of approaching heaven. The image screen was once highly coloured, and would have been visible for miles over the low roofs of the city. Some of the carved figures have been altered over the years, but we believe they originally represented the kings and prophets of the Old Testament, and the twelve apostles whom Jesus Christ appointed as the beginning of his Church. Above these are places for singers or instrumentalists to stand and give the impression of angels singing. Over the battlements of this heavenly city are crowded a host of carved faces. This screen was the finishing touch to the great rebuilding of Exeter Cathedral, begun under Bishop Bronescombe (d. 1280) and completed under Bishop John Grandisson (d. 1369).

The visitors' entrance may be at either the West or the North Door. In any case, go round the Cathedral to see the north tower more clearly. Although the two Norman towers look at first sight identical, they are subtly different. On the north side, St Paul's Tower is slightly taller and more austere, whereas St John's Tower, on the south, is more usually bathed in sun and is more delicate in its appearance. Both are highly decorated with zig-zags and roundels, and are excellent examples of Norman building.

The Interior

The best place to see the building as a whole is from inside the Great West Door. The building is all of a piece. Its present appearance is the result of an astonishing century of hard work, following a consistent pattern from beginning to end. As you look eastward you see the pointed architecture of the thirteenth and fourteenth centuries. Surprisingly, there is no hint of the Norman towers, so obvious from outside. They were part of the building begun by Bishop Warelwast in 1114. But less than a century after the Norman building was finished it was largely rebuilt as you see it today. As he finished the new Cathedral, Bishop John Grandisson proudly informed the Pope that Exeter now had 'a church to rival all the cathedrals of England and France'. Grandisson included a chapel for himself (2) in the thickness of the wall to the right of the main door, its windows half hidden among the carvings. His tomb has been destroyed, but some of the carving remains – especially that showing Christ risen from the dead, in the height of the vault. Sometimes in summer it is open for you to visit.

The Cathedral is, as it has always been, the centre of a community devoted to prayer and worship, who care for a building of the utmost beauty, and fill it with magnificent music and colour. In addition to the Dean and the Chapter of canons who lived around the Cathedral, there were dozens more staff (the vicars choral, chantry priests, clerks and choristers) who shared in the Cathedral's round of worship. The Cathedral was like a town within the town. Today, the Chapter includes lay people as well as clergy, and this larger body reports to the Cathedral Council and a College of Canons. There is, however, a clear continuation with the organisation set up in 1225.

Beneath your feet are the graves of many people of the distant past. Above you, the arches are like the trees of paradise. Many people notice that Exeter Cathedral seems larger inside than outside. This is largely due to the unexpected width of the building in comparison with its height, and the way the roof draws the attention upwards and away towards the east. The roof is Exeter's chief glory, and because the towers stand to each side, the arches and ribs extend to make an unbroken pattern to the almost invisible East Window. The vista is broken by the organ case, standing above the stone screen. But even before the present seventeenth-century organ case was made, there was an interruption to the view, because this was where a large cross used to stand, dominating the whole scene. The message is that your journey is not over yet, that the heart of the

(Left)
Many schoolchildren visit the Cathedral to make music and share in services.

(Right)
View of the length of the Cathedral.

building is beyond, at the end of the avenue of tree-like arches over your head.

This large pillared space is the nave of the Cathedral, used for major acts of worship as well as for concerts. The pillars were built of Purbeck stone from Dorset in the fourteenth century, their colour bluish and contrasting with the main building stones quarried in Devon from Beer and Salcombe Regis. Many of the records of the day-by-day progress of the building survive in the Cathedral Archive. The colours of the stone are made all the more striking by the other particular beauty of Exeter – the light. The designers made the most of their skill in making the windows as large as possible, so that in winter or summer there is endless variety of light and shadow. They also created windows with inventive designs, making circles, arches, squares, stars and innumerable other geometrical shapes in the stone tracery. The West Window, especially when seen against the evening sun, shows their mastery of design as much on the big scale as on the small. They wanted to show how God, in making all the variety of the world, was nevertheless the same God in everything. In creating the most beautiful possible building, they intended that we should sense the God who fills it and is even greater than it.

From the inside of the main door, to your left and up a couple of steps, is the Chapel of St Edmund (3), enclosed by a chunky wooden screen. This is the chapel of the former Devon Regiment, and contains various memorials to those who served with it. There are many military memorials and standards throughout the Cathedral, commemorating those from Devon who served their country throughout the world. The most elaborate memorial, on the north side of the nave, is to the Bengal Lancers at the time of the rebellion in 1857. By the noted sculptor Marochetti, it shows the huge mortality from disease in those days.

On the west wall is a memorial to R.D. Blackmore, the Devon-born author of *Lorna Doone*, one of the most famous novels of the West Country.

As you walk down the nave, use a mirror trolley to admire the bosses high above you along the length of the roof. A noticeable one, not far from the main door, depicts the death of St Thomas Becket, Archbishop of Canterbury in 1170. Becket's murder caused a sensation throughout Europe, and Canterbury became the most popular pilgrimage destination in Britain. One of the knights who murdered him at Canterbury was from Devon. Later on your visit you will see a model of a roof boss, showing just how massive these carved keystones are – they each weigh some two tonnes. The bosses in the nave are much brighter than those further east, as a result of modern repainting. The fashion in conservation now is for less bright colour.

More fine carving is to be seen between the arches and above the columns. Above you on your right as you leave the West Door is one of

(Above) Roof boss in the nave with Henry II's knights murdering Thomas Becket, Archbishop of Canterbury.

(Above) The pulpit.

several depictions of the coronation of the Virgin Mary. The idea of the humble woman who gave birth to Jesus being crowned as queen of heaven was especially inspiring to those who designed the Cathedral. Foliage is carved everywhere, and human heads emerge unexpectedly.

Also on the right is the font (4), made in 1684 of Sicilian marble. One of the windows along this side commemorates the Blitz which destroyed so much of Exeter in 1942. Despite a direct hit, the Cathedral survived.

Halfway down the nave, high on the left side, is the unique minstrels' gallery (5), carved with fourteen angels playing instruments. In fact this is a screen in front of a room which acts as an echo chamber, and it is pierced so that sound can float out into the nave below. At Christmas and other times choristers still use this to create a remarkable disembodied sound, and recently organ pipes have been placed there to give extra power at this end of the Cathedral for hymns and recitals.

The pulpit (6), on the north side, was designed by Sir George Gilbert Scott, who carried out the restoration work at Exeter in the 1870s. This is in Scott's typically florid style, depicting martyrs for the faith, including St Alban and St Boniface. Occupying pride of place is a carving of the death of Bishop John Coleridge Patteson, an East Devon man who became the first Bishop of Melanesia in the South Pacific and was martyred in 1871.

Above the pulpit is one of the lively painted carvings attributed to Roger, who was the Master Mason around 1300. This one depicts an acrobat, a minstrel, and a dog.

All around the nave, covering the stone seats, are the Exeter Rondels. These cushions are the work of devoted volunteer workers in tapestry, and tell the story of Exeter Cathedral from its beginning to modern times. The names of the bishops and the deans accompany the scenes through the centuries. There is a booklet available in the shop to help your enjoyment of this unique work.

(Left) Water is poured into the font as a baby is baptised into Christian life.

(Right) View of the minstrels' gallery.

On the north wall, near the pulpit, past musicians of the Cathedral are commemorated. One memorial is to the musical prodigy Matthew Godwin, who died aged seventeen in 1586.

Sunday worship usually centres on the movable altar in the nave, but sometimes there is staging for concerts or other activities as you approach the pulpitum (screen). Here the hollowed-out towers on each side make a broad space – the crossing – which is often the largest unencumbered area of a cathedral. Two fine seventeenth-century brass chandeliers are lit on special occasions. The pulpitum itself (7) used to be a solid barrier so that you could see the quire only through the gate. Scott opened the back of the pulpitum to allow a glimpse of the quire beyond. Altars are placed, as they were long ago, under the arches, and recently the Cathedral has become home to a pre-Reformation wood-carving of the crucifixion of Christ, now above the north altar. It shows in vigorous carving both the rampageous soldiers and the grieving friends of Jesus, among them his swooning mother and St Mary Magdalen with her long hair. It was probably made in the Netherlands in about 1500, and came to the Royal Albert Museum in Exeter for careful restoration and eventual loan. It gives some idea of the type of decoration that was swept away at the Reformation. In the pavement beneath this altar is the grave of Thomas Bracton, an early expert in English law.

(Left) Detail from the Exeter Rondels.

(Below) Altarpiece housed in the pulpitum.

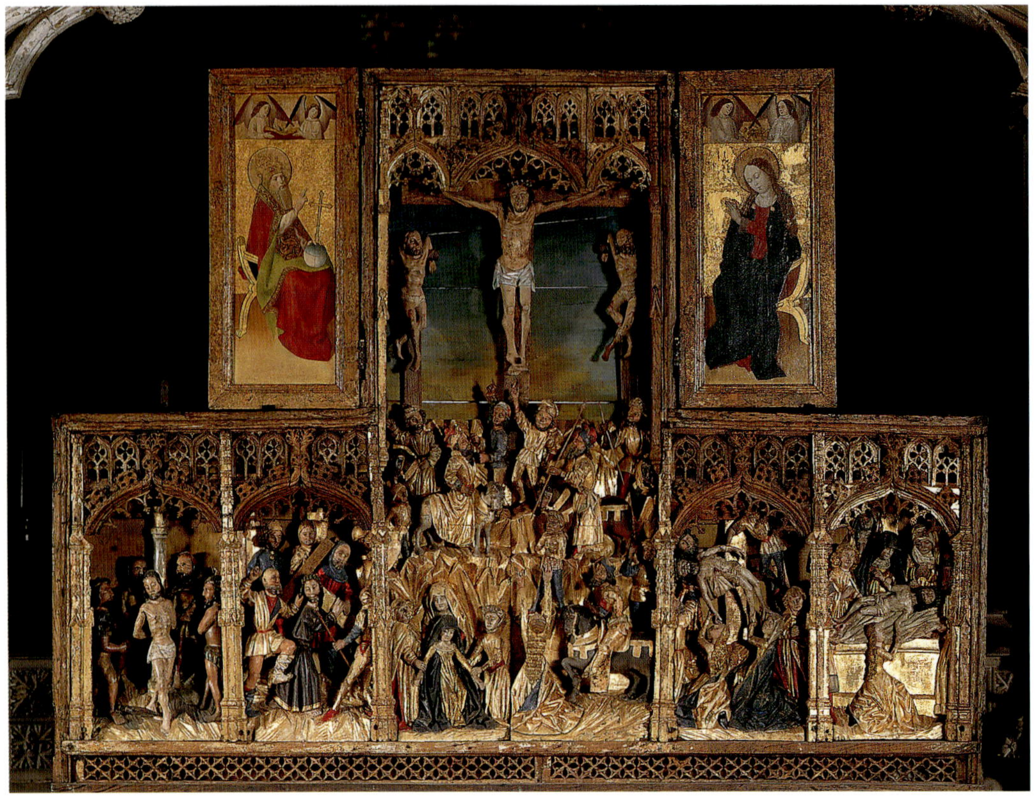

(Above) Candles are lit in front of an icon at the pulpitum.

The pulpitum was superbly carved after 1316 while Master Thomas of Witney was the master mason responsible for the rebuilding of the nave. In the seventeenth century, paintings of scenes from the Bible were made along the top of the pulpitum in a lively but quaint style. At each end are two of several icons in the Cathedral. These, of Jesus Christ and of St Peter, were 'written' by John Coleman, an icon-writer in residence at the Cathedral in 2002.

(Right) Matthew Godwin monument.

(Above) The Cathedral cat exits the north tower via a centuries-old round hole, designed specifically for the purpose.

The spaces under the towers are the transepts, and the transept to the north is the home of the Exeter clock (8). It was placed here in 1484, but has been restored several times since. Old wooden doorways lead into stairs in the towers from here, and in the one below the clock you can see a round hole. This allowed a cat to enter the tower to deter rats and mice from infesting the towers. A penny a week was provided in the fifteenth century to feed the cat. On the west wall, notice the

(Above) Window by Sir Ninian Comper, depicting Christ walking on the water (1940s).

(Far left)
The Exeter clock.

(Left)
Late mediaeval wall painting of the Resurrection.

(Right)
Twentieth-century carving of St Christopher.

(Far right)
Mediaeval carving, reminding us of our mortality.

life-size statue of James Northcote R.A. (d. 1831) by Sir Francis Chantrey.

In the north-east corner is the Chapel of the Holy Cross (8), built for Masses to be said in memory of Precentor Sylke who died in 1508. In the fashion of his time he is carved in all the pitifulness of death, his image made all the more wretched by having been seriously damaged. Above the chapel there survives a rare wall painting of Christ rising from the dead, with the burial of Christ depicted in a modern reconstruction below.

The Chapel of St Paul (9) is next to the Sylke chantry. Its screen was delicately restored in the early twentieth century with the addition of some exquisite saints, St Christopher and St Nicholas among them. The work was done by woodcarver and stonecarver Herbert Read, to whom the Cathedral owes so much. Some of the mediaeval paintwork survives. Ancient fragments of glass were gathered into the window of this chapel in about 1920. It also contains a modern icon, a gift from the cathedral in Bahrain.

Through a door in a wooden screen between the pulpitum and the north transept is the walkway, or north quire aisle, leading around the east end of the Cathedral and encircling the quire. Processions enter the quire through the Golden Gates in the centre of the pulpitum, ascending towards the high altar. In some services they pass around the quire aisles, encircling the heart of the building and catching glimpses of the high altar.

The Cathedral contains numerous memorials to bishops of Exeter over the centuries. The first major one, on your left, is to Bishop Carey (d. 1626), whose tomb of coloured alabaster matches Bishop Cotton's, which you will pass on the south side.

The Chapel of St Andrew and St Catharine (10) houses regular exhibitions on the theme of Justice, Peace, and the Integrity of Creation. The altar of St Andrew, the fisherman brother of St Peter, is the place where we commemorate HMS Exeter, which was sunk in 1942 off Java, and those who died or were imprisoned as a result of that loss. A window by Sir Ninian Comper shows Christ walking on the water and giving a saving hand to St Peter when he tried to imitate his master.

Back in the quire aisle, notice the fine Purbeck marble tomb on the right, rather squeezed under an arch. This is possibly the tomb of Bishop Marshall (d. 1206), which you can see better from the quire. On the left is another carving of a corpse, more complete than that of Precentor Sylke, and tilted towards you for stronger effect.

This macabre carving was put here to remind us to amend our lives ready for heaven while we have time.

A little further on the right is the simple stone of the tomb of Bishop Lacy, who died in 1455. After his death, visits to this tomb were believed to give healing, and a number of small wax fragments have survived (now in the Cathedral Library), representing the limbs of those who had been healed here.

Towards the east end two splendid tombs face each other. They are of two brothers, Sir Richard and Bishop Walter Stapeldon (11). Richard's tomb, on the left, is damaged, but shows his horse being restrained by his page. That of his brother was thoroughly restored in the nineteenth century. As treasurer of England under Edward II, he was the victim of riots towards the end of the unpopular king's reign. This tomb, which he had created in his own lifetime, is in a proud position near the high altar. Stapeldon's carved effigy looks up to the ceiling just above him, where the figure of Christ is painted and looks down on him in turn.

At the corner on the left is the intricately carved Chapel of St George (12), created as a chantry chapel where prayers were said for the soul of Sir John Speke (d. 1518). Sir John lies in full armour in his chapel, a romantic figure of a Christian knight from the age which much honoured the patron saint of England and chivalry. Also here are the cross and figures by Justin Knowles (2002). Made from cerulean crystal in the Czech Republic, they look light in spite of their weight, and light passes through them almost perfectly. The cross, recalling Jesus's death, frames the stone carving of Jesus's birth immediately behind. The cross's simple shape also recalls the many granite crosses on and around Dartmoor. Some of the carved statues which were often hacked away at the Reformation have survived, including one, outside by the door, of Mary as a child being taught by her mother, St Anne.

The Chapel of St John the Evangelist (13), next to the Speke chantry, also takes up the chivalric theme. An overpowering memorial to Sir Gawen and Lady Carew (1589) projects from the north wall, covered in heraldry. Their nephew Sir Peter is depicted below, like a knight of the thirteenth century. In this chapel is the brass of Canon William Langton, who died in 1414. Much ancient glass has been gathered and reassembled in the east window of this chapel.

To your right is the effigy of Bishop Stafford (d. 1419). His effigy was later placed in an elaborate gilded monument with flying angels and inscriptions (14). Some of the graffiti in the soft alabaster are centuries old. On a pillar outside this chapel is a wooden case made to contain service books in a time when the value of a bound book was enormous. A similar case can be seen beyond the Lady Chapel.

The Lady Chapel is dedicated to 'Our Lady', St Mary, and is the place where the morning prayers of the Cathedral are said. This is also the place where people come to sit and be quiet. They often leave prayers outside the chapel to be used in the daily services of the Cathedral. In 1942 the dark glass was blown out, and now it is a far lighter place than it used to be. It is dominated by the splendid tracery of the East Window, which was filled in 1948 with a busy design by

(Right) The Chapel of St George contains cerulean crystal sculptures made in 2002.

(Above) *Cross in the Lady Chapel.*

Marion Grant showing the triumph of right over wrong, told through Mary's life. The theme of Mary as the mother of Jesus Christ is taken up in other details in this chapel. To the left of the doorway, in a niche, is a tender wooden sculpture from the early sixteenth century of the Bethlehem shepherds, one of them playing a pipe, with their sheep. In one of the windows on the south side a panel of German glass has been inserted, with the same theme of Mary with her mother as in the carving by the St George chapel. Again this is the subject of the wood-carving to the right of the door, which is probably Flemish and dates from the sixteenth century.

Over the years this chapel has been used for various different purposes, and was turned back into a chapel in the nineteenth century when the east end was remodelled as we now see it.

(Right) *Tomb of Dorothy, Lady Dodderidge.*

The present cross and the candlesticks are the work of John Hayward (1970). On the south side are alcoves, filled since the early seventeenth century with two effigies. One is of Judge Dodderidge (d. 1628), but the finer tomb is that of his wife, Dorothy, who is shown wearing a sumptuous dress. The inscription says that when God raises us to new life in heaven he will make us anew, as a clockmaker reassembles a clock to tell the time of eternity.

Opposite Lady Dodderidge a modern copy of a traditional icon has been placed, and visitors light candles and offer prayers here. Below the icon is a fine tombstone, probably that of Bishop Bartholomew (d. 1184).

The finest effigy in the Cathedral lies between the Lady Chapel and the Chapel of St Gabriel, opposite Bishop Stafford. This figure of Bishop Bronescombe (d. 1280) is carved out of basalt, and has survived with its original colouring, though like Bishop Stafford's effigy it has been placed in a later, brilliantly gilded monument (15). The bishop is shown wearing the magnificent robes of a prelate of his time. Two angels, carrying his shield, look upwards expectantly, so that the figure seems ready for life rather than death.

The Lady Chapel was the first part of the Cathedral to be rebuilt in 1270, and the rebuilding continued to the west, transforming

View of the Chapel of St Gabriel, with the effigy of Bishop Bronescombe in the foreground.

Green Man boss, near the Lady Chapel.

the earlier building as it went. Its style set the pattern which was then continued throughout the Cathedral, complete with the ribbed pattern of the vaults and the lively bosses.

Look up outside the Lady Chapel to see more fine bosses. The finest is that showing the Green Man, a decorative image popular in the Middle Ages. There are several depictions of the Green Man in the Cathedral – this one shows two human faces among leaves.

Just beyond the Lady Chapel, up to the left, is a surviving wall painting of the early sixteenth century. Covered in plaster at the Reformation, and partly obscured by a late seventeenth-century memorial to a local merchant, it shows the Virgin Mary ascending to heaven while God the Father and Jesus look down in welcome. The nine orders of angels sing as Mary rises through the battlements of heaven, her hands meekly folded in prayer. The design has been reproduced below it to make it clearer.

The Chapel of St Gabriel (16) has the best surviving painted screen in the Cathedral. Not only has the paint survived on the stonework, but the paintings on the screen panels and the wooden doors are still bright. To the left, the angel Gabriel comes to Mary announcing that she is to give birth to the Messiah. On the door itself is the popular saint of the Middle Ages, St Apollonia, the patron saint of dentists. She carries a tooth in a pair of long pincers.

Sixteenth-century wall painting depicting the Assumption of the Virgin.

Detail of St Apollonia on the wooden door of the Chapel of St Gabriel.

(Left)
The icon of the Virgin of Tenderness in the Lady Chapel, 'written' for the Cathedral in 2002, shows Mary the mother of God full of compassion for the troubles of the world. Many people come to this part of the Cathedral for quiet and prayer.

(Below)
Fifteenth-century glass depicting Jesus on the cross.

In this chapel a light burns in front of the aumbry (wall cupboard), where a small amount of the sacrament of bread and wine is kept throughout the year. The design of the aumbry, and the cross and candles on the altar, is by Louis Osman (1964). These works insist that Christ has come into a bitter and brutal world, of machinery and tortured metal. Christ is shown on a cross barbed by nails, his body reduced to taut sinews, but leaning forward to show a face (or is it a heart?) of warmth and love. Above this is a more conventional portrayal of Jesus in his suffering, in the form of a panel of fifteenth-century glass put above the altar. He gazes sorrowfully down towards the aumbry.

The altar has been reconstructed using what is probably the main altar of the mediaeval Cathedral. At the Reformation it would have been used for a flagstone, the altar being a wooden table, but it was reinstated here in the mid-twentieth century. The huge window on the south side of this chapel is a complete survival of mediaeval glass, such as would once have been found throughout the building.

Next to the Chapel of St Gabriel is another

chantry chapel, dedicated to St Saviour (17), meaning Christ. It was planned to match St George's Chapel, and was the chantry of Bishop Oldham who died in 1521. It is covered with his badge of owls, one of them with the inscription 'Dom' coming from its beak, punning on his name ('Owldom'). A promoter of education, at Oxford and in his native Manchester, Bishop Oldham is honoured every year by a visit from Manchester Grammar School and the laying of a wreath. The bishop lies in a brightly repainted tomb on the south side, looking towards the altar as if to join in with the communion services. Above the altar is a much-broken carving of a theme popular in the later Middle Ages – the Mass of St Gregory. A drawing is preserved in the chapel to make clearer what is being depicted. A story was told of Pope Gregory the Great having a vision that the bread and wine he was using to celebrate Mass turned into the real, suffering body of Jesus. The reformers of the sixteenth century disliked the popes and the idea that communion bread and wine could be turned into the real body of Jesus, so the sculpture was damaged and left as a sign of the superstition that had been destroyed.

The south quire aisle suffered the most damage from the bomb which hit the Cathedral on 4 May 1942. Many monuments here show signs of having been reassembled after the war. A survivor of the bomb, but very worn, is the large floor brass just outside Bishop Oldham's chantry. It shows Sir Peter Courtenay (d. 1409) – see the illustration on the wall above it. A little way along the ambulatory on the right are two knights lying in niches, cross-legged and in armour. It is not clear who they are. One of them may be a member of the Ralegh family, but they have lost nearly all the colour and decoration that they would originally have had.

(Right, above) *Tomb of Bishop Oldham.*
(Right) *A bomb-damaged memorial.*

Opposite them is the memorial to General John Simcoe, who helped to found Toronto. He served with distinction in the American War of Independence and established Fort York, where Toronto now stands, in a then uninhabited stretch of forest by Lake Ontario. He died in the Cathedral Close and is buried in Wolford Chapel, at his family home near Honiton. This memorial is the work of the noted artist John Flaxman. Not only is the portrait head of Simcoe finely done, but the main inscription is flanked by two fine full-length figures. To the left is a British soldier resting on his musket; to the right, a figure of a Native American with his tomahawk lowered.

Outside the Chapel of St James (18) you will see the statue of Jesus the Good Shepherd, created by Roseanne Keller (1995). This figure, pulling a sheep from danger, is modelled on a shepherd the artist saw on Hatterall Hill in South Wales.

During the Second World War, on the night of 4 May 1942, a high explosive bomb landed on the Chapel of St James. Nothing was left of the original chapel, nor its undercroft. As well as the destruction of much of the masonry, the wooden screen opposite was smashed. Indeed, damage was caused all around, especially to the glass of windows throughout the Cathedral. The destruction of Exeter was a retaliation for the earlier destruction of Lübeck and, when rebuilt, this chapel was the scene of reconciliation (recorded in an inscription) with the President of the City of Lübeck. As this chapel is that of the Devonshire and Dorset Regiment, its origins in the ruins of war make a connection with the peacekeeping duties of the modern army in the context of NATO and the United Nations. Also preserved here in a case is the roll of the Wessex Division, created in 1944 to carry through the campaign after D-Day through northern France. In it served many people from the south west of England.

The appearance of the chapel is largely as it was before the bomb. A contemporary touch was brought to the carvings next to the windows, one showing George Down the Master Mason when the chapel was rebuilt. As you leave the chapel, notice the carvings on either side of the arch. One shows the then head virger's cat, Tom. Tom lost his eye in a fight with an owl over a rat. The rat is carved opposite.

The screen into the quire opposite this chapel was painstakingly reassembled by Herbert Read after the war, who described it as the 'biggest jigsaw puzzle in the world'. Newer wood can be made out among the carefully harvested fragments of the old screen, but the general impression is of undamaged mediaeval work.

(Left) Early nineteenth-century memorial to General John Simcoe.

(Above) Carved head of George Down, the master mason responsible for the post-war rebuilding of the Chapel of St George.

(Right) View of south quire aisle.

(Above) View looking up at the bishop's throne.

(Left) Nineteenth-century carving in the quire by Brindley and Farmer.

(Right) Mediaevel misericord with carving of an elephant.

The screen leads into the heart of the Cathedral, the quire, the destination of all processions, the place where the daily choral services are held and where the Cathedral's beauty is concentrated. To your left are the choirstalls. These were commissioned from a London firm by George Gilbert Scott in the nineteenth century, when he remodelled the whole quire. The stalls at the rear incorporate the mid-thirteenth-century misericords – seats which, when tipped up, reveal a ledge on the under side on which you could prop yourself during very long services. These ledges are often elaborately carved, and those at Exeter are among the earliest in England. The most famous of them, depicting an elephant, is exhibited behind the bishop's throne. You can see it as you leave the quire.

Girl choristers sing in the quire.

The back row of stalls is occupied on great occasions by the prebendaries (clergy of the diocese who are appointed to the College of Canons); the Bishops of Crediton and Plymouth, who are the suffragan (deputy) bishops of the diocese; members of the Cathedral Foundation; and honoured guests. The carved stalls at the east ends of the stalls and on either side of the Golden Gate are occupied by the four chief office-holders of the Cathedral – the Dean, Chancellor, Precentor, and Treasurer. The stalls have elaborate canopies, and many carvings of angels, people from the Bible, animals, fish, and birds.

To the south is the lofty bishop's throne (19). Designed by Thomas of Witney from 1312 and carved by Robert of Galmpton, it is one of the finest specimens of mediaeval woodwork to be found anywhere. It has lost its ancient statues and colouring, but kept some beautiful flying angels. It was dismantled during the Second World War and so saved from destruction. Herbert Read carved a new statue of St Peter to stand in its centre, modelled on the much-loved Bishop William Cecil (d. 1936). The seat inside the throne is a fine painted chair of the reign of Elizabeth I. This is the cathedra, the seat of authority which the bishop occupies when he attends major services at the Cathedral.

In 1688 Prince William of Orange landed at Brixham with a large army. He spent a week in Exeter, weighing up whether or not to advance to London to confront James II, with all the possibility of a civil war. But then James fled, William and Mary were crowned in his place, and the Protestant establishment was assured for the next few generations both here and in Ireland. William occupied the bishop's throne (the Bishop and the Dean kept well away) while his declaration of peaceful intent was read.

(Left) View looking east towards the high altar.

(Right) Looking up at the quire vaulting.

(Far right) Fine foliage carving in the quire.

(Above) Detail of the marble floor, designed by Sir George Gilbert Scott.

(Left) The brass lectern in the quire.

Near the throne in the centre of the quire is a brass lectern (reading desk), in the form of an eagle gripping the world and carrying the Bible. From here readings are given when services are held in the quire. It was given to the Cathedral in 1690, but is probably fifteenth century.

If you turn towards the east, where the steps rise towards the high altar (20), you will see what would have been a dramatic climax for the mediaeval visitor to the Cathedral. Behind the altar a rich wall of statues, enriched with silver, rose to the base of the East Window. During the Reformation this area was stripped of its splendour, and for three hundred years underwent various adaptations until Scott's restoration. Scott tried to recapture something of the original decoration with an alabaster altar-piece which stood until the late 1930s, when it was found to be unstable. When it was taken down the present view through to the pillar and the Lady Chapel was revealed, and the taste of the time led the Chapter to decide not to reinstate it. It has found a home in the parish church of Heavitree, Exeter, while the Cathedral has a simple cross casting a shadow on the bare wall above.

Scott carefully restored the whole of this area, redesigning the marble floor, raising the steps, redecorating the ceiling and paying particular attention to the sedilia (ceremonial seats for the clergy), on the south side of the altar (21). Their canopies hint at the decoration of the disappeared altar screen. They retain some delicate original colouring and, apart from the modern statues, they look unrestored. The statues are of the Cathedral's founders.

The carvings between the arches and in the bosses of the roof are among the best in the whole Cathedral. The designs of the leaves are full of variety and liveliness. Everywhere there are human heads and symbols of the faith. Look out particularly for the coronation of the Virgin above the high altar, a crucifixion and a mermaid.

(Right) Sedilia in the quire.

(Left) The East Window in the quire, depicting Jesus in Mary's arms, flanked by St Barbara and St Martin.

The East Window is one of the Cathedral's glories. Its design is rather later than that of the other windows, but some of the glass filling it is among the earliest. At the top the figures of Isaiah, Moses, and Abraham date from 1304. At its centre is a graceful figure of Mary holding the child Jesus. Around her are arranged various saints, including, to the upper left, the local martyr St Sidwell (carrying a scythe), to whom one of Exeter's ancient parish churches was dedicated. Next to her and of the same date (1291) are St Helena and on the other side St Edward the Confessor and St Edmund, with the arrows with which he was martyred. This ancient glass was reset in this window in the eighteenth century, and survived the Second World War by being taken down and stored.

Leave the quire by the way you came, noting the elephant misericord behind the bishop's throne.

On the left side as you turn right along the quire aisle are some interesting memorials. One is of the Treasurer Edward Cotton, dated 1675, leaning out with a look of intelligence. The memorial to Bishop Lavington shows he was a severe critic of John Wesley's Methodism – he found the excitement caused by Wesley's preaching suspect and dangerous.

Further on is the memorial to Bishop Cotton, matching that to Bishop Carey in the north quire aisle. Emblems of mortality surround him – a cherub blowing bubbles, Time holding an

(Right) Fourteenth-century carving of swans in mourning, from the Courtenay monument in the south transept.

hourglass, and skulls. Beyond this, half hidden in a corner, is the grand memorial to Bishop Weston (d. 1741), who before he was Bishop of Exeter had been a schoolmaster at Eton. A graceful baroque recording angel points to his inscription while kneeling on a pile of books.

Pass through the doorway and turn left into the south transept to reach the Chapel of St John the Baptist (22), with its plain stone altar. From the chapel door you can see the intertwined necks of two swans at the feet of a knight and his lady. The memorial is of Hugh Courtenay Earl of Devon (d. 1376) and his wife Margaret de Bohun (23).

In the corner of the transept, near the St John's Chapel, is a row of wires connected to the bell chamber above the wooden roof high over your head. These enable the bells for the daily service to be chimed without having to take the long journey to the bell-chamber. The thirteen bells of Exeter are hung so as to be rung in a circle, and by weight they are second only to those at Liverpool Cathedral. There is a further huge bell of 1484 hanging in the north tower, which is chimed on the hour by the clock. At Christmas, Easter, and Pentecost the Cathedral bells are rung in the early morning, before the first services of the day. They have wonderful names such as Grandisson, Stafford, Pongamouth, Purdue, Little Nine o'Clock, and Doom.

(Above) Green Man carving above the organ loft.

The west wall of the south transept is covered with the thirty-two foot diapason pipes of the organ. Their characteristic sound is a deep rumble, and they were put here when the organ was rebuilt in 1891. There has been an organ in the Cathedral since before the Reformation, but if it survived the sixteenth century it was demolished when the Civil War came to Exeter. The city was held for the king, and was considered safe enough to be a home for Queen Henrietta Maria with her children. One of them, Henrietta, was baptised in the font (not the present one) in 1644. Eventually, the city was fiercely fought over, being finally occupied by the forces of Parliament.

In spite of promises that the Cathedral would be spared damage when the city yielded after the siege, the Parliamentary soldiers broke the organ up. The Chapter was disbanded, and the Church of England went into hiding. The Cathedral suffered considerable damage. A wall was built at the pulpitum to make room for two churches – Great Peter to the west for the Independents, and Little Peter to the east for the Presbyterians.

(Left) One of the Cathedral bells.

The organ.

After Cromwell's death and the crowning of Charles II, the Dean and Chapter were restored to office and rebuilt the organ. The case by John Loosemore remains, dated 1665. The organ itself, however, was splendidly rebuilt by the famous 'Father' Willis in the late nineteenth century. After further improvements made by the firm of Harrison & Harrison more recently, it is now one of the finest organs in the region and is used not only for services throughout the year, but for regular recitals.

Through the door at the corner of the transept you pass towards the Chapter House by a narrow flight of stairs. Here is where the Chapter meets each month to govern the Cathedral. It is also the 'parish hall' of the Cathedral. Its high roof is richly carved with angels, put there after a fire in 1413. This was when the Chapter House was enlarged upwards to its present height. You can see from the walls how it seems to be one building on top of another. The pointed arcade around the wall is filled with sculptures by Kenneth Carter, dating from 1974. Those on the north side show the creation of the world described in the Book of Genesis. Those on the south show the coming of Jesus Christ and the healing of human life, from the coming of the angel to Mary at the west end to the resurrection of Christ and the fall of the devil at the east.

Enter the Cloister Garth by the door at the foot of the stairs. This was where the cloister stood until after the Civil War. It was demolished to make room for a cloth market, built on wooden pillars, for the sale of Exeter's chief manufacture at that time – baize cloth. The hall survives, the pillars embedded in the wall on the south side of the garth, but the building itself was converted to houses. So extreme was the need for housing that the whole of this area was soon surrounded by dwellings, their chimneys smoking against the walls and windows of the Cathedral, and their back yards filling much of the space. Not until the nineteenth century were they mostly removed, so that now only one range survives, on the west side, housing the Cathedral offices.

Schemes to reconstruct the cloister were advanced during the nineteenth century, and a start made to the designs of John Loughborough Pearson, the architect of Truro Cathedral. Pearson built a section of cloister closely modelled on what had stood before, and above it a fine room to house the Library. Today the Refectory is housed in the cloister room he designed, and you can see the excellent quality of

Fifteenth-century angel in the Chapter House roof.

his work, which incorporates some fragments of the cloister found as the old houses were demolished. The Archives and part of the Library are housed above.

To your right as you come into the Cloister Garth you can see the round Norman door from the Cathedral into the demolished cloister. The cloister extended between the buttresses along the Cathedral wall, with a complicated system of drains for rainwater and vaults set into the walls which still leave their traces. At the west end is another door from the Cathedral into the cloister. The gap still remains where the money ran out for Pearson's rebuilding scheme. He left the arches unfinished as a hint of what might one day be done, if ever the funds were available, to rebuild the cloister across the front of the Chapter House and to the door into the Cathedral.

Cloister window in the present Refectory, with eighteenth-century glass by William Peckitt of York.

There is one part of the Cathedral which is separate from the rest – the Library. To reach it (open on weekday afternoons between 2 pm and 5 pm) you must go towards the Refectory and turn left by the side of the Chapter House. Down some steps and across a yard you come to a door in the part of the Bishop's Palace occupied by the diocesan office. Inside, a bell for the Library will gain you admittance.

In the Library are exhibited some of the treasures of the Cathedral. The Exeter Book, preserved in a case, was presented in 1050 by Edward the Confessor to the first Bishop of Exeter, Leofric. It contains a considerable proportion of the surviving Anglo-Saxon literature, clearly written in an unfaltering hand, in the form of poems and riddles. The Exeter Domesday is an early version (1086) of the great survey carried out in the reign of William the Conqueror, and covers the south west of England in great detail. Many important books were donated to the Bodleian Library in Oxford in 1602, but Exeter's Library still contains many fine volumes, some of which are usually on display, including a large number of medical books. Recently the Library has developed a modern collection to support the needs of people studying for work in teaching and preaching in today's church life. Among other treasures displayed is Bishop Grandisson's ring.

The Library is staffed largely by volunteers, as is the Cathedral shop. The daily life of the Cathedral relies heavily on the enthusiasm of volunteers, to welcome and guide visitors, to decorate the Cathedral with flowers and needlework, and assist with many aspects of its daily running.

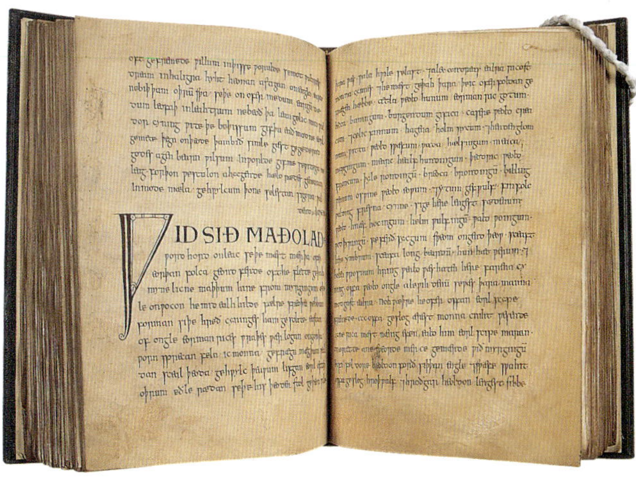

(Right) The Anglo-Saxon Exeter Book in the Cathedral Library.

Further Reading

For further reading about the Cathedral, a good general guide is *Exeter Cathedral, a short history and description* by Audrey Erskine, Vyvyan Hope, and John Lloyd (Exeter 1998). *Exeter Cathedral, a Celebration*, edited by Michael Swanton (Exeter 1991) has fine illustrations and contributions on many aspects of the building and its contents, as well as a guide to further reading. *Exeter Engraved Vol 2* by Todd Gray (Exeter 2001) contains many engravings of the Cathedral. Other booklets on various aspects of the Cathedral can be found at the Cathedral shop.

The official website has a wealth of detail about the Cathedral, and can be found at: www.exeter-cathedral.org.uk

Rooftop view.

Exploring the City

There is much to see in Exeter. Red Coat Guides offer free tours throughout the year, starting from the Cathedral Close near the Royal Clarence Hotel. The Royal Albert Memorial Museum in Queen Street has important collections, with fine displays connected with Exeter's history. The Roman city walls, the Norman castle, the mediaeval Guildhall, and the historic Quayside are all only a short walk from the Cathedral.

For full details, contact:
Exeter Tourist Information Centre
Civic Centre, Paris Street, Exeter EX1 1JJ.
Tel: 01392 265700. Fax: 01392 265260.
Website: www.exeter.gov.uk

Tomb of the 2nd Earl of Devon, 1376, in the south transept.

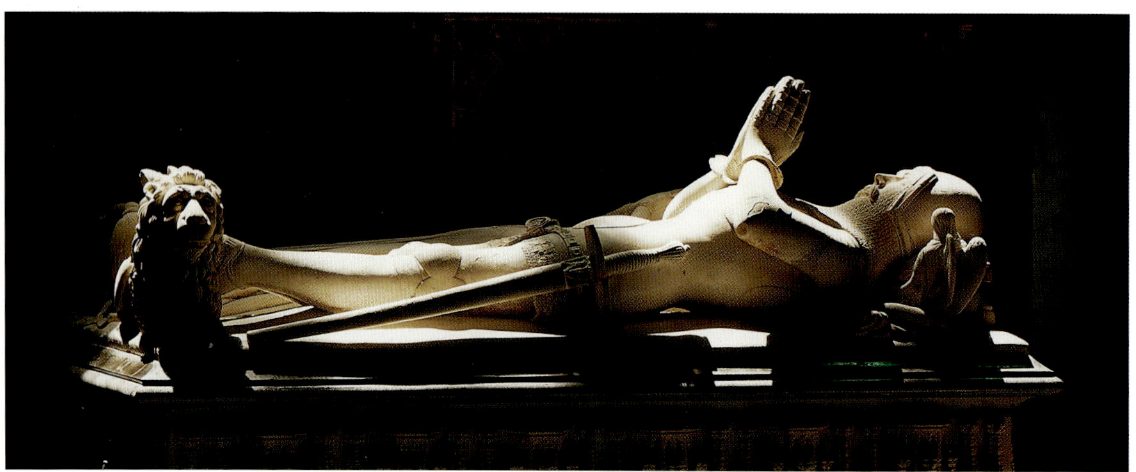